The Legend the Bluebonnet

Pat Cusick Ripton

Illustrated by Diana Kizlauskas

Rigby®

A Harcourt Achieve Imprint

www.Rigby.com
1-800-531-5015

The sun was hot, and nothing could grow on the dry land. The Wisest Comanche talked to Mother Earth.

"Save your people, Mother Earth. Our land is dry, and we cannot find food. We are very unhappy. We need your rain to help us.

"If the rain does not come, all the plants will die. But if you hear us and send rain, the land will turn green. The rivers will flow again, and the buffalo herds will come back."

On the evening of the third day, the Wisest Comanche heard a voice from the hills.

"The Earth is dying because the Comanche people take what they need from Mother Earth, but they do not give anything back. If you all want to eat again, one of you must offer me a gift. One of you must give me the thing that you love the most.

"You must place the gift in the fire and burn it. After you spread its ashes in the wind, I will send rain."

The Wisest Comanche built a fire and called his people together.

"Mother Earth has asked for a gift," he said. "One of you must offer the thing that you love the most. Then it will rain, and we will have food again."

"I will give this bow and arrow," said a young man. "I made it from the branch of a tree that grows in a forest far away."

"I will give this beautiful, warm blanket," said a woman. "I made it with soft cloth and feathers."

All of the Comanche people talked about the special things that they owned. But one by one they took their gifts back to their homes.

That night the Wisest Comanche lay down to sleep. At midnight he heard footsteps.

He discovered a young Comanche girl named She-Who-Is-Alone near the fire. She was holding a doll in her arms, and the Wisest Comanche listened as she talked to her doll.

"Beautiful doll, you are the thing that I love the most because my mother made you before she died. She used the softest cloth. She painted your eyes with blueberry juice, and she put blue beads on your belt. She put three blue feathers in your hair."

The child held her doll in front of the
fire and looked at it for the last time.

"If I do not offer my doll as a gift and
help my people, then we will all die. I
must help my people."

Then she placed her doll on the fire and
watched it burn and slowly disappear.

When the ashes were cold, She-Who-Is-
Alone collected them and threw them
into the wind. Then she lay down and
fell asleep. It began to rain.

In the morning, after the rain had
passed over the land, the Wisest Comanche
turned to watch the sunrise. He looked out
over the hills and wondered whether what
he saw was real or a dream!

The hills looked very different now. The land was not dry and bare. Blue flowers covered the hills, and everything looked alive again.

She-Who-Is-Alone woke up and smiled when she saw the flowers.

"Mother Earth has received your gift," the Wisest Comanche whispered to the child.

"Yes, Mother Earth is happy," she said. "She is speaking to all the people, telling us that we must take care of the Earth."

Just then they heard a blue jay sing.
The Wisest Comanche and She-Who-Is-
Alone followed the bird from hill to hill,
looking at the blue flowers that grew there.

When they got home, the Comanche
people greeted She-Who-Is-Alone. They
thanked her for her gift.

Every spring Mother Earth fills the hills and valleys of Texas with beautiful blue flowers. They remind us of the gift the young Comanche girl offered Mother Earth. We call these flowers bluebonnets.